P9-DWD-968

THE SUN & MOON SIGNS LIBRARY
PISCES

FEBRUARY 19 – MARCH 20

JULIA AND DEREK PARKER

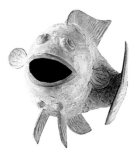

Photography by Monique le Luhandre
Illustrations by Danuta Mayer

PRENTICE-HALL CANADA, INC.
SCARBOROUGH, ONTARIO

Dedicated to Doreen Foad

First published in Canada in 1992 by
Prentice-Hall Canada, Inc.
Scarborough, Ontario

A DORLING KINDERSLEY BOOK
Editor **Tom Fraser**
Art Editor **Ursula Dawson**
Managing Editor **Krystyna Mayer**
Managing Art Editor **Derek Coombes**
Production **Antony Heller**

Computer page make-up Patrizio Semproni.
Photography p 10 CM Dixon/British Museum; p 11 National Gallery,
London/Bridgeman Art Gallery, London; p 16 Tim Ridley. Stylist pp 28-29
Lucy Elworthy. Illustration pp 60-61 Kuo Kang Chen. Jacket illustration
Peter Lawman. With thanks to Carolyn Lancaster and John Filbey.

First published in Great Britain in 1992 by
Dorling Kindersley Limited, 9 Henrietta Street London WC2E 8PS
Copyright © 1992 Dorling Kindersley Limited, London
Text copyright © 1992 Julia and Derek Parker
Reprinted 1994
A CIP catalogue record of this book is available from the
National Library of Canada
ISBN 0-13-678970-6

Reproduced by GRB Editrice, Verona, Italy
Printed and bound in Hong Kong by Imago

CONTENTS

INTRODUCING
PISCES

PISCES, THE SIGN OF THE TWO FISHES, IS THE TWELFTH SIGN OF
THE ZODIAC. THE PISCEAN CHARACTER IS MARKED BY A
NATURAL QUIRKINESS, AND THIS IS SYMBOLIZED BY THE FISH
SWIMMING IN OPPOSITE DIRECTIONS.

The two fishes that symbolize this sign are connected by a cord held in their mouths and are always portrayed swimming in opposite directions. They suggest a strong characteristic of the Piscean personality: Pisceans often decide on one line of action, and then take precisely the opposite course. Not surprisingly, this may impede your progress through life.

Traditional groupings
As you read through this book you will come across references to the elements and the qualities, and to positive and negative, or masculine and feminine signs.

The first of these groupings, that of the elements, comprises fire, earth, air, and water signs. The second, that of the qualities, divides the Zodiac into cardinal, fixed, and mutable signs. The final grouping is made up of positive and negative, or masculine

and feminine signs. Each Zodiac sign is associated with a combination of components from these groupings, all of which contribute different characteristics to it.

Piscean characteristics
The water element is a powerful source of emotion and, because Pisces is of the mutable quality, you are likely to be flexible in your views. You are full of marvelous creative potential, but may sometimes doubt yourself. If you lack self-confidence, you will need continual support and encouragement in order to develop and fulfill your promise.

Neptune, the god of the sea, is the Piscean ruling planet. Although you are probably very kind, Neptune's influence can persuade you to seek easy ways out of difficult situations. All too often this involves deceit. The sign is negative and feminine, so Pisceans tend to be introverts.

ARIES
PISCES
TAURUS
AQUARIUS
GEMINI
CAPRICORN
CANCER
SAGITTARIUS
LEO
SCORPIO
VIRGO
LIBRA

FIRE

CARDINAL   EARTH

MASCULINE   MUTABLE   AIR

FEMININE   FIXED   WATER

The Zodiac Wheel

The relationship between each Zodiac sign and the traditional astrological groupings is made clear within the Zodiac wheel. As you read through this book you will also discover references to polar, or opposite signs, and these, too, can be easily worked out by referring to the wheel.

MYTHS & LEGENDS

THE ZODIAC, WHICH IS BELIEVED TO HAVE ORIGINATED IN
ANCIENT BABYLON AS LONG AS 2,500 YEARS AGO, IS
A CIRCLE OF CONSTELLATIONS THROUGH WHICH THE
SUN MOVES DURING THE COURSE OF A YEAR.

The ancient Babylonian name for this constellation was *kun*, meaning "the tails." This title referred to the tails of the two fishes that were associated with the goddesses Anunitum and Simmah, who once represented the rivers Tigris and Euphrates. The great Roman writer Manilius, who set down a number of astrological myths, gives us a stronger link with the sign of Pisces. It actually derives from the earlier literature of the Greek writer Hyginus, who wrote one of the first works on mythology.

Typhon
Made in the sixth century B.C., this terracotta figure shows the monster Typhon.

Venus and Cupid

Hyginus's story involved Venus and Cupid, who were the Roman versions of the Greek Aphrodite and Eros.

The former was the goddess of love, who was said to preside over a love that bonded all living creatures, and to inspire all of Nature's creations. The latter was her son by her husband, the graceless and ugly god Vulcan. Cupid was originally conceived as the god who was responsible for harnessing the different elements of the universe, allowing life to develop. Clearly there is a link between the role of Cupid and that of his mother. From these abstract origins, he came to be seen as an immortal child with the ambition to infect both mortals and the gods with the virus of love. Cupid is often shown firing arrows from a bow.

Venus and her son Cupid

This representation of Venus, the goddess of love, and her son Cupid was created in the 1500s by Agnolo Bronzini.

These arrows were invested with the power to stir great passion in the hearts of all those that they struck.

Typhon the monster

Far removed from the notions of love and beauty associated with Cupid and his mother was Typhon, the youngest child of Mother Earth and the largest monster ever born.

From the thighs downward he was nothing but coiled serpents, and his arms, which were said to span a hundred leagues in any direction, ended in countless serpents' heads. As his name suggests (it is the root of the word *typhoon*), Typhon was said to be responsible for any unusually strong winds.

Venus and Cupid are transformed

According to the myth, Venus and Cupid were strolling along the banks of the Euphrates one day when they were confronted by an enraged Typhon. In order to evade him they immediately turned themselves into fish, and swam off rapidly in opposite directions. To commemorate the event, Zeus, king of the gods, placed the constellation now known as Pisces in the heavens.

The two fishes

Even today, the fishes used to represent the sign face in different directions, although they are connected by a single golden cord. This perfectly indicates the perversity that is such a powerful characteristic of Sun sign Pisceans. They will almost inevitably argue strongly for one course of action only to eventually decide to take precisely the opposite course.

SYMBOLISM

CERTAIN HERBS, SPICES, FLOWERS, TREES, GEMS, METALS, AND
ANIMALS HAVE LONG BEEN ASSOCIATED WITH PARTICULAR
ZODIAC SIGNS. SOME ASSOCIATIONS ARE SIMPLY AMUSING, WHILE
OTHERS CAN BE GENUINELY USEFUL.

PINKS

Plants
*Dandelions, lime-flowers, mosses, lichens,
waterlilies, and pinks – in fact most
plants that grow in Piscean colors – are
all associated with this Sun sign.*

MOSS

Trees

The lime, birch, mulberry, chestnut, ash, oak, birch, and all trees that grow near water are ruled by Pisces.

BIRCH

SAGE

CHESTNUT

Herbs

Herbs ruled by Cancer and Sagittarius come under the influence of Pisces. They include sage and saxifrage.

Spices

No spice is particularly associated with Pisces, but coriander and cinnamon are sometimes mentioned.

CORIANDER

CINNAMON

PISCES
SYMBOLISM

FISH MOULD

Gem
The Piscean gem is traditionally said to be the colorless moonstone. Magical properties are often attributed to it.

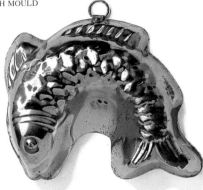

MOONSTONE

Metal
The Piscean metal is platinum, but traditional astrology also mentions tin and titanium, which emit the entire color range of the spectrum and are therefore well suited to Piscean taste.

PLATINUM NUGGET

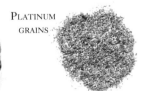

PLATINUM GRAINS

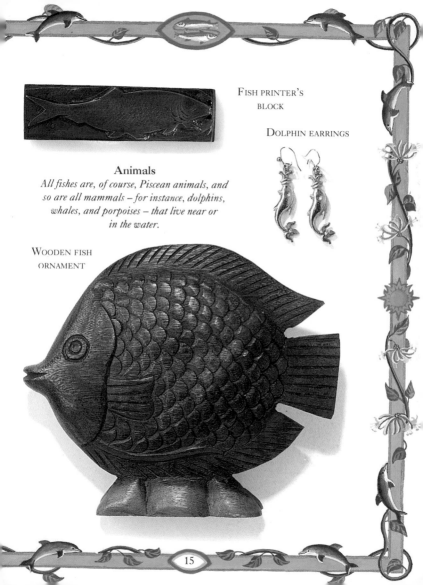

FISH PRINTER'S
BLOCK

DOLPHIN EARRINGS

Animals

*All fishes are, of course, Piscean animals, and
so are all mammals – for instance, dolphins,
whales, and porpoises – that live near or
in the water.*

WOODEN FISH
ORNAMENT

PISCES
PROFILE

PISCEANS OFTEN SEEM TO WALK AROUND IN A DREAM, FAR AWAY
FROM THE BUSTLE OF EVERYDAY LIFE. BECAUSE THEY CAN
BE FORGETFUL AND MAY HAVE THEIR MINDS ON HIGHER THINGS,
THEY HAVE A TENDENCY TO DRESS CARELESSLY.

Many Pisceans stand with their feet crossed, like a fish's tail. This distinctive stance is often noticeable at social gatherings or at cocktail parties.

The body
It is not difficult to recognize Pisceans who have an undisciplined and unhealthy approach to life. They will tend to look overweight, and have flabby, shapeless bodies and rather dull eyes. However, Pisceans who decide to dedicate themselves to some grueling physical activity like skating or dancing will appear to be fitness itself, even if they possess typically pale Piscean complexions. Piscean creative potential and inspiration will be likely to keep them practicing at the barre long after many other people would have decided to give up.

The Piscean face
Pisceans often have gentle eyes and unstyled, natural-looking hair.

The face
Pisceans will either style their hair heavily, or lean in quite the opposite direction and leave it in its natural state. You will tend to frown if you are worried or confused. The eyes are a dominant feature in many Pisceans and will probably appear to be gentle, perhaps showing a capacity to be very emotional. A dominant feature is very often a drooping line at the corner of the eye. Your nose is likely to be well shaped and from small to medium in size; some Pisceans tend to have noticeably high bridges to their noses.

16

The Piscean stance
Pisceans frequently stand with both feet crossed, forming the distinctive shape of a fish's tail.

Style
The Piscean image is romantic. Many Piscean men love to own velvet jackets, while Piscean women can look stunning whether they are dressed in a Paris creation or simply have a length of fabric pinned around them. Unless career commitments force you to dress conventionally, you will probably have an extremely original image and may like wearing unusual antique clothes. You are unlikely to become too great a slave of fashion, unless some aspect of your life demands it.

You will look your best wearing soft fabrics such as wool, and you may veer toward an ethnic look.

Your feet are very likely to betray the fact that you are a Piscean. Perhaps without even realizing it, you could have a tendency to wear rather broken down, well-worn shoes.

In general
A softness and gentleness, an eagerness to sympathize, is very apparent on first meeting a typical Piscean. There is nothing pushy

about these people. They will always listen to others with interest, and their eyes reflect the emotions of the people they are conversing with. As has been said, the eyes are nearly always a very dominant Piscean feature. Piscean women will probably not take long to discover that they can use their eyes to their advantage. Many will develop a range of subtle expressions and inflections.

PISCES
PERSONALITY

PISCEANS ARE SAID TO BE THE POETS OF THE ZODIAC. WHILE
NOT ALL OF THEM WILL SPEND HOURS PENNING
VERSES TO THEIR LOVERS, MANY DO SEEM TO SHARE
THE INSPIRATION ASSOCIATED WITH THIS ART.

Words such as unworldliness, dreaminess, and inspiration are all frequently used to describe head-in-the-clouds Pisceans; but so are charity, kindness, and helpfulness. You probably have a great willingness to ease other people's burdens.

Many Pisceans find it difficult to face up to reality. While you may have an ability to identify with suffering and often actually the means to do something about it, you may also have a tendency to retreat into your own little world. You could be a recluse.

At work
It should come as no surprise to find that the characteristics mentioned above may influence your choice of career. You would do best to find work that offers plenty of variety, and that does not force you to labor through the same hours every day. A predictable job might provide you with a sense of security, but it could prove to be stifling. Well-defined regulations or guidelines may provide you with a useful sense of direction, and you should have no problems in following them. Try to study and learn from the way that your superiors handle authority and manage to cope with decision making.

Your attitudes
Many Pisceans need peace and quiet. This can mean the quiet of the cloister or, ironically, it can cause you to disconnect yourself from the everyday world by blasting loud music into your ears through a personal stereo. Either way, you will probably find the experience restorative.

The overall picture
The symbolism of the sign is opposite and represents a true Piscean problem. Just as the two fishes of Pisces swim in opposite directions, Pisceans will often fail to

Neptune rules Pisces

*Neptune, the Roman god of the sea, represents the Piscean
ruling planet. It can make its subjects idealistic, imaginative,
and sensitive, but also careless, indecisive, and deceitful.*

act in their own best interests. It may be that a certain lack of self-confidence often prompts you to decide on one line of action – and to then do just the opposite. Unfortunately, you may find this happening just when you are attempting to act particularly positively and assertively. You must be careful not to rely on excuses in order to avoid starting new projects. If, for example, you say that you have no time to start something new, you are probably actually falling victim to a lack of self-confidence – whether or not there is an element of truth in your excuse. You must make an effort to harness your complete potential.

PISCES
ASPIRATIONS

IT IS POSSIBLE THAT YOU DO BETTER WORKING BEHIND THE SCENES
THAN OCCUPYING A HIGH-PROFILE POSITION. IF YOU
LEARN TO INTERPRET YOUR IMAGINATION PRACTICALLY,
IT WILL BE A VALUABLE ASSET TO YOU.

Painting

*Many Pisceans are very creative,
and the work they can produce as
painters may be both beautiful and
imaginative. They should not
underestimate their potential.*

WATERCOLOR
PAINTS AND BRUSHES

PRISON
OFFICER'S KEYS

Prison work

*If you work in the prison
service you will be very
sympathetic to your
charges. The ability to
listen to problems is a
great asset in
this profession.*

CLOWN'S MASK

Medical research
The motivation to help others and reduce suffering can attract Pisceans to medical research.

The theater
Pisceans are natural mimics and have an attractive sense of humor. This may lead to a career as a comedian or a mime.

MICROSCOPE

The shoe trade
Pisces rules the feet, and some creative people of this sign become successful shoe designers, while others find the fitting and selling of shoes rewarding.

SHOE TREES

HEALTH

PISCEANS TEND TO BE UNDISCIPLINED, AND YOU MAY SOMETIMES
NEGLECT YOUR HEALTH AND GENERAL WELL-BEING.
YOU WOULD THEREFORE BE WISE TO NOTE THE FOLLOWING
SUGGESTIONS AND WARNINGS.

The feet are ruled by Pisces, so people of this sign often have problems with this area of their bodies. Exercise sandals are the ideal footwear for them. More serious than problem feet may be your inclination to fall back on forms of escapist behavior, such as drug-taking and excessive drinking. This is because you often have difficulties facing up to reality, as well as a self-deceptive attitude that encourages you to take any easy way out of a problem situation. Sun sign Pisceans should recognize their vulnerability and call upon other, stronger

areas of their personality to counter it. The Piscean system often tends to be sensitive, so other people's reactions or bad attitudes can have an adverse physical effect on you.

Your diet
You may benefit from supplementing your diet with Ferrum phosphate (ferr. phos.), which is a combination of iron and oxygen that enriches the blood and soothes inflammation.

Taking care
Interestingly, many Sun sign Pisceans do not respond well to medically prescribed drugs – an allergy to antibiotics is common. Alternative medicine could be the solution to this problem in some cases.

Cucumber
Cucumbers and melons are among the foods traditionally linked with Pisces.

Astrology and the body

For many centuries it was not possible to practice medicine without a knowledge of astrology. In European universities, medical training included information on how planetary positions would affect the administration of medicines, the bleeding of patients, and the right time to pick herbs and make potions. Each Zodiac sign rules a particular part of the body – from Aries (the head) to Pisces (the feet) – and textbooks always included a drawing of a "Zodiac man" (or woman) that illustrated the point.

PISCES AT
LEISURE

EACH OF THE SUN SIGNS TRADITIONALLY SUGGESTS SPARE-TIME
ACTIVITIES, HOBBIES, AND EVEN VACATION SPOTS.
ALTHOUGH THESE ARE ONLY SUGGESTIONS, THEY OFTEN WORK
OUT WELL FOR PISCEANS.

POSTAGE STAMPS

Travel
*You will enjoy wandering aimlessly on one of the
small Mediterranean islands or in the Sahara.
Portugal and Scandinavia may also be favorite
destinations. You will be eager to try local food,
but should watch your digestion.*

Flying
*The idea of "getting away from it
all" is restorative to Pisceans.
They will become excited at the
thought of taking off in an
airplane to enjoy
vacations.*

1916 AVIATOR'S MAPS

Dance
*Lyrical dance movement
can provide a non-
competitive, steady,
rhythmical, and therefore
rewarding form of self-
expression for Pisceans.*

Flower arranging

Sensitivity, artistic flair, and a love of nature are Piscean traits that often make people of this sign talented flower arrangers.

CHICKEN WIRE
AND FLOWERS

FLY-FISHING HOOKS

Fishing

The peace and quiet of a solitary afternoon's fishing allows a Piscean to calm down and escape from the rat race.

BALLET SHOES

PISCES IN
LOVE

PISCEANS GIVE A GREAT DEAL OF THEMSELVES TO THEIR LOVERS.
THIS CAN EITHER BE MARVELOUS FOR BOTH PEOPLE
INVOLVED, OR IT CAN MEAN THAT THE PISCEAN WILL SACRIFICE
TOO MUCH AND BECOME A DOORMAT.

Many Sun sign Pisceans have a tendency to view the world through rose-colored glasses when they are in love. They often delude themselves. You may have to develop a much thicker skin than you naturally possess, and make sure that you are not taken in by a combination of flattery and good looks. Your tendency to idealize your prospective partner may sometimes cause you to either ignore or conveniently overlook the true picture.

Deceptiveness, the main Piscean fault, can surface in another way: because Pisceans hate to hurt others, they may sometimes tell white lies in order to take the easy way out of a difficult situation.

As a lover
Pisceans give a great deal of themselves to their lovers. This can either be marvelous for both people involved, or it can mean that the Piscean will sacrifice too much and become a doormat. They also often instinctively know what their partners are feeling and thinking. This is a useful, if sometimes embarrassing, asset. You are capable of sharing and maintaining an extremely rewarding,

long-lasting sex life, which will be a great source of pleasure and fun. If you have partners who are able to recognize and encourage the full development of your potential, and above all else help you to become more self-confident, every aspect of your life will be rewarding.

Types of Piscean lover

One group of Pisceans is not quite as gushing or gullible as has been suggested. People belonging to a second group have a rather special glamour. They need to retain their independence and might tend to be a little cool and distant toward their partners. While enjoying love and sex, they may delay making a total commitment. A third type of Piscean is a true Piscean, who will easily recognize all of the general comments made so far. Yet another group is made up of enthusiastic, passionate Pisceans, who do not find this area of their lives to be particularly complicated. They contribute a great deal to a partnership once they settle down. People in the final group are very sensual, passionate, and affectionate. They usually need to have a great deal of emotional and financial security within their relationship.

PISCES AT
HOME

YOU LIKE YOUR HOME TO BE A HAVEN OF PEACE AND TRANQUILLITY.
PALE BLUE OR GREEN SOFT FURNISHINGS WILL REFLECT
YOUR QUIET GOOD TASTE, AND A TROPICAL FISH AQUARIUM MAY
ADD TO THE OVERALL RELAXED ATMOSPHERE.

The majority of Pisceans like to live near a source of water, ideally in a coastal area. If this is not possible they may design their own small haven of peace and tranquillity in even the most run-down or unappealing type of area. While doing so they may become heavily involved with the local community, and perhaps lend their enthusiastic support to various charitable groups or conservationist organizations.

Bronze vase
A vase or jug in the shape of a fish is not uncommon.

A Piscean home is always guaranteed to be a most interesting place to visit.

Furniture

Comfortable furniture is essential, but because Pisceans tend to be artistic and creative, the appearance of pieces is also important. If you are short of money, the look of your secondhand furniture may be enhanced by imaginative repairs and repainting. Settees and beds are generally jumbo-sized and very soft. You use them to retreat into your own blissfully private, imaginative world. Scrubbed pine is popular for kitchen and dining tables, and you may own a large china

Subtly patterned cushions
Pretty designs and soft colors will feature heavily in any Piscean decorative scheme.

cabinet or cupboard which will be full to the brim not only with cups and plates, but all types of clutter.

Soft furnishings

Piscean invention and imaginative creativity are expressed in the creation of unusual cushions and small items of furniture that enhance more important pieces. Patchwork, screen printing, and sculpting all find their place in the Piscean home.

The curtains and drapes will be either chintzy and floral, or rather shimmery, giving a waterlike appearance. Moiré silk in pale pastel shades of green, blue, or sometimes silvery gray, often features in the Piscean decorative scheme. Floor coverings are generally heavily textured or thick-piled, with Greek flokati rugs being special favorites.

Decorative items

Any paintings that you choose probably have a romantic air, and those that are psychologically restorative and calming are usually preferred. Lighting comes from shaded lamps placed in discreet corners. There may be an aquarium in your home; this will serve as both a container for extoic tropical fish and a purely decorative feature. Pisceans are often good at flower arranging, and dried flowers and bowls of potpourri may be prominently displayed around your home.

Lamp and books
Generous lampshades and piles of books typify the Piscean home.

THE
MOON
AND
YOU

THE SUN DECREES YOUR OUTWARD
EXPRESSION, YOUR IMAGE, AND MANY
IMPORTANT PERSONALITY TRAITS. THE
MOON, ALTHOUGH MERELY THE EARTH'S
SATELLITE, IS ASTRONOMICALLY THE
SECOND MOST IMPORTANT BODY IN THE
SOLAR SYSTEM. FROM THE SIGN THAT IT
WAS IN AT YOUR BIRTH, IT INFLUENCES HOW
YOU REACT TO SITUATIONS, YOUR
EMOTIONAL LEVEL, AND, TO A CERTAIN
EXTENT, WHAT YOU HAVE INHERITED FROM
YOUR PARENTS AND ANCESTORS. AFTER
FINDING YOUR MOON SIGN IN THE SIMPLE
TABLES ON PAGES 56 TO 59, TURN TO THE
RELEVANT PAGES AND TAKE A STEP
FORWARD IN YOUR OWN SELF-KNOWLEDGE.

THE MOON IN
ARIES

YOUR FIERY, EMOTIONAL, AND LIVELY MOON LENDS A STRONG
POSITIVE FORCE TO YOUR PISCEAN PERSONALITY. DO
NOT BE AFRAID TO EXPRESS THIS FREELY. IT ADDS STRENGTH
AND ASSERTIVENESS TO YOUR RESPONSES.

While Aries is strong, positive, and assertive, Pisces is gentle, tender, and not at all pushy. The influence of your fiery Moon gives you a powerful source of physical and emotional energy.

Self-expression
You initially respond boldly to challenges, but could later have second thoughts that eat away at your self-confidence and cause you to backtrack. Aim to move forward steadily, and to allow the gentler, more conscientious elements of your Piscean Sun to be stimulated by the strong forces of your Arien Moon.

Romance
You possess both the fiery, expressive emotion of Aries and the deep, intense emotion that derives from Pisces. In addition to these qualities you are passionate and are likely to fall in and out of love very quickly.

Your Arien Moon probably makes you more resistant to being upset than most Pisceans, and you have the ability to detach yourself once you realize that an affair is over. You have what it takes to enjoy a rewarding, fulfilling relationship, although the worst Arien fault, selfishness, could surface at times.

Your well-being
The Arien body area is the head, and you could suffer from more than an average number of headaches. These are probably the result of worry and tension. There can be a link between headaches and slight kidney disorders, so it is worth getting a medical checkup if they persist.

Like many people with an Arien emphasis, you are usually in a hurry. Because of this, you could be somewhat accident-prone; consciously take care, particularly when working with sharp tools or hot dishes.

The Moon in Aries

Although you probably enjoy sports and exercise, you do need to watch your diet. You may not worry much about it, and Piscean haste could encourage you to consume an excessive amount of junk food.

Planning ahead

You may well have an enterprising spirit that could supply you with a useful second income. However, seek financial advice when you have money to invest. Otherwise you may make serious mistakes. These will be the result of combining soft-hearted Piscean traits with those of an over-enthusiastic Arien.

Parenthood

You will be a sympathetic parent and will be anxious to see your children make progress. You will not find it difficult to keep up with their ideas. Try not to continually change your mind, or your children will not know where they stand with you.

THE MOON IN
TAURUS

YOUR PISCEAN KINDNESS AND SYMPATHY DO NOT ALWAYS WORK
TO YOUR COMPLETE ADVANTAGE. LISTEN TO YOUR
SENSIBLE AND PRACTICAL TAUREAN MOON, AND MAKE AN
EFFORT TO CURB POSSESSIVE REACTIONS.

The water element of your
Piscean Sun and the earth
element of your Taurean Moon blend
well. You are far more reliable and
stable than many Sun sign Pisceans.

Self-expression
The Moon is traditionally well placed
in Taurus, which means that its
influence on you is particularly strong.
It gives you backbone and acts as a
marvelous anchor to your personality,
calming what can sometimes be a
turbulent spirit.

When challenged, you face up to
reality with great practicality. You can
be very firm and decisive, and should
always follow your most deep-rooted
instincts and intuition.

Both Pisces and Taurus have
considerable creative potential, and
Taurus is particularly appreciative of
beauty. If you enjoy embroidery,
pottery, craftwork, and music, you
should develop these interests.

Romance
It is very important for you to have a
secure background. Material security
does not always interest Pisceans, but
your Taurean Moon puts an emphasis
on both it and emotional security.

You will relax into and enjoy a
relationship with a partner who you
feel you can trust. You are a powerful
source of affection and sexuality,
being sensual and passionate. When
you feel secure, these qualities do
much to enhance your relationship.

The worst Taurean fault is
possessiveness, and you will
sometimes try to own your partners.
Be aware that they may need some
independence within a relationship.

Your well-being
The Taurean body area is
traditionally said to cover the throat
and neck. Your colds are likely to
begin with a very sore throat and end
with a cough. Make sure that you

The Moon in Taurus

keep the appropriate medicines on hand so that you can relieve any discomfort as soon as possible.

Taurus loves rich and often sweet food, so you may have a tendency to gain weight, especially since Pisceans can suffer from a similar difficulty. Discipline yourself into a reasonable diet and a regular exercise routine.

Planning ahead

You have an above-average capacity to cope with finance; it is far better than that of most Pisceans. If you do

seek financial advice, you will be surprised at how close your own ideas are to those of your adviser. You will probably want to own your own home as early in life as possible.

Parenthood

You will be stricter with your children than most Pisceans and will discipline them sensibly. They will know where they stand with you, but you may have to make a conscious effort to understand their problems if you are to avoid the generation gap.

THE MOON IN
GEMINI

YOUR MOON HELPS YOU TO RATIONALIZE YOUR POWERFUL PISCEAN
EMOTIONS. PISCES AND GEMINI ARE BOTH DUAL SIGNS,
WHICH MEANS THAT YOU ARE NATURALLY VERSATILE. YOU MUST
CURB SUPERFICIALITY AND BE CONSISTENT.

The chances are that you will be a free-thinker with a flexible, open mind. This is largely because Pisces and Gemini are both mutable signs. You are also extremely versatile, enjoying a great variety of interests, and finding it easy to converse with many different kinds of people on a wide range of subjects.

Self-expression

You are a marvelous communicator and are able to get your ideas across very easily. It is, however, entirely possible that you may alter your opinions at a moment's notice.

You respond to proposals with a flurry of words, showing great enthusiasm if you like what is put to you and producing a variety of hastily invented excuses if you do not. Because of your Piscean Sun, you may lack self-confidence and could try to cover the fact by being nervously talkative. Try to take your time, and remember that a few well-chosen sentences can make a far better impression than a tumble of words.

Romance

You are probably unlikely to be completely overwhelmed by your emotions. You may rationalize your feelings, especially when you first fall in love. Try not to restrain your emotions. A certain measure of skepticism from your Geminian Moon is valuable, but do not let it smother the heart's affections. Bear in mind, too, that friendship and a good measure of intellectual rapport are as essential for you in a long-term relationship as a good sex life.

Your well-being

The Geminian body area covers the arms and hands. Yours are therefore vulnerable, perhaps to minor accidents. The Geminian organ is the lungs. Do not allow a cough to hang

The Moon in Gemini

on for more than a few days before resorting to prescribed antibiotics. Anyone with a Geminian emphasis should not smoke.

Restlessness can affect your health, but a relaxation discipline could help counter this. If your metabolism is fast, you will be less likely than most Pisceans to suffer from weight gain.

Planning ahead
Pisceans are often not particularly adept at finance, and money tends to burn holes in Geminian pockets.

Resist sob-stories from those who wish to borrow your money, and get financial advice, especially before leaping into get-rich-quick schemes.

Parenthood
You will be both a loving and a very lively parent: youthful and alert, and with few generation gap problems. You may need to be a little more strict than you are if your children are to know precisely where they stand with you. Remember that they need a sense of security.

THE MOON IN
CANCER

BOTH PISCES AND CANCER ARE SIGNS OF THE WATER ELEMENT,
SO YOUR EMOTIONS, INTUITION, AND IMAGINATION
ARE HIGHLY REFINED. YOU MUST TRY TO CHANNEL THEM
IN A CONSTRUCTIVE AND POSITIVE WAY.

With Pisces and Cancer both being water signs, you have some very powerful, emotionally oriented forces within your personality. The Moon rules Cancer and is at its strongest and most influential from that sign. It will have a deep effect on your personality.

Self-expression
You have considerable strength and determination; when you are challenged in any way, an immediate and powerful self-defensive system springs into action. You respond strongly, either kindly and sympathetically or sharply, according to your opinions and the way you feel.

Both Pisces and Cancer enhance your powers of imagination, and you should always try to express your creativity, perhaps inventively. If you do not, your imagination may work overtime in a negative way. Your instincts and emotions are very powerful. If you feel that you should take a particular line of action, you will probably be right to do so. But always calm yourself down before doing anything important.

Romance
You will be a very passionate, sensual lover and will make a wonderful partner in a long-term relationship or marriage. You know how to please your lover both in and out of bed, and will not find it difficult to achieve sexual fulfillment. Make sure that you do not nag your partner, and remember that in expressing your love, it can be all too easy for you to create a claustrophobic atmosphere.

Your well-being
The Cancerian body area covers the breasts and chest. It is therefore advisable for Cancerian women to be particularly diligent in examining their breasts regularly, although there

The Moon in Cancer

is, of course, no connection between the Zodiac sign Cancer and the disease with the same name.

You enjoy good food and may well be prone to weight gain. Try to discipline yourself into getting regular exercise, perhaps swimming.

Planning ahead

Those with a Cancerian emphasis have a very shrewd business sense and are talented at making the most of what money they have. You will have some good ideas about what to do with your money, but your Piscean Sun may detract from them, and you could be overly generous to charity. Seek professional advice when you have money to invest.

Parenthood

You will be among the most sensitive and caring of all Piscean Sun and Moon sign parents, and will stimulate your children's imagination and encourage their efforts. You will be strict enough to discipline your children as and when necessary, but warm and comforting when they are distressed. Make sure that you do not get too sentimental; this could lead to problems with the generation gap.

THE MOON IN
LEO

YOU HAVE MARVELOUS POTENTIAL, CAN RESPOND POSITIVELY TO
MOST SITUATIONS, AND ARE PROBABLY BETTER ORGANIZED
THAN MOST PISCEANS. AT TIMES, YOU MAY BE PRETTY BOSSY –
BUT THAT CAN BE USEFUL TO A SENSITIVE PISCEAN.

There are some very vivid contrasts between the qualities of Pisces and Leo, but this is still a stunning combination. It makes you a fascinating individual with exciting, dynamic potential.

Self-expression

Your fiery Moon contributes a wonderfully positive enthusiasm when you are challenged. No doubt you are far more self-assured than many people of your Sun sign, and certainly much better organized. You could also be more self-confident and, at times, perhaps rather bossy.

Pisces and Leo are probably the two Zodiac signs with the most creative potential. Pisceans often do not have the confidence to develop this quality, but your Leo Moon will help you to overcome your inhibitions. Always aim to achieve the highest standard and to make a dramatic impact, whatever you do.

Romance

Like Pisces, Leo is a very emotional sign. You express your passion with great feeling and are a very ardent lover. You make a caring partner, but probably fall in love often and suffer heartbreak just as much as, if not more than, other Pisceans.

You are very sensitive and, when hurt, will instinctively creep into your lair and lick your wounds in private. It is probable that you will want to look up to and admire your partner. You will always be a splendid power behind a throne, but you also need to share it. Avoid any inclination to dominate your partner.

Your well-being

The Leo body area covers the back and spine, and yours may be vulnerable. If you work at a desk you might benefit from an ergonomic chair. Exercise will also keep the back and spine in good order.

The Moon in Leo

The Leo organ is the heart, and it also needs exercise. Work out at a health club, or find some form of exercise that expresses your sense of drama and creative talent.

Planning ahead

Unlike most Pisceans, you enjoy doing things in style and spend freely on luxuries. Since you are also generous by nature, you will need to earn a relatively high salary.

You will probably be inclined to invest in fairly safe, well-established companies making quality products. Make sure that you get your decisions confirmed by a professional financial adviser before you invest large sums of money.

Parenthood

Leo is a sign that is traditionally related to parenthood. You will make an enthusiastic parent, always ready to praise and encourage your children.

While you should not suffer from too many generation gap problems, you should try to allow your children to develop their own interests, and refrain from forcing your ideas upon them. Do not expect them to achieve goals that have always eluded you.

THE MOON IN
VIRGO

PISCES AND VIRGO ARE POLAR OR OPPOSITE ZODIAC SIGNS, WHICH
MEANS THAT YOU WERE BORN UNDER A FULL MOON.
INNER DISCONTENT AND RESTLESSNESS MAY BOTHER YOU, BUT DO
NOT BE WEIGHED DOWN BY BAD FEELINGS.

We all have a tendency to express the attitudes of our polar, or opposite, Zodiac sign. Every sign has its partner across the horoscope; for you this is Virgo, and since the Moon was in this sign when you were born, the polarity is expressed in a very interesting way.

Self-expression

Virgo is an earth sign, and this element blends well with the water element of Pisces, making you practical and rational. You are an excellent communicator, and enjoy a good, lively discussion or argument.

It is possible that you may not be very self-confident, and a certain shyness can inhibit you. You are very good at covering this up, perhaps by being overly talkative, but your lack of self-confidence is very deeply rooted. When asked to organize something, or when an opportunity for promotion occurs, you may well

not be willing to accept it. It is entirely possible that you are seriously underestimating your abilities.

Romance

Lack of confidence could also emerge when someone makes a romantic approach to you. You have a delightful natural modesty, but do not let it inhibit you to the extent where you lose the opportunity for what might be a rewarding relationship.

Also bear in mind that the worst Virgoan fault is to be overcritical. Beware of a tendency to nag your partner; it could be devastating.

Your well-being

The Virgoan body area covers the stomach, and since those with a Virgoan influence are very prone to worry, the physical effects usually center around an upset stomach, pains, and cramps. You need a high-fiber diet, and may be sympathetic to

The Moon in Virgo

vegetarianism. Perhaps you are less prone to weight gain than many Pisceans. This could be because you have a high metabolism and therefore a lot of nervous energy to burn. Exercising will alleviate restlessness and encourage sleep. You will favor outdoor sporting activities.

Planning ahead

You are careful with money, and may be too worried about losing it to take any undue risks. You would be wise to go for safe investments with steady growth and to obtain financial advice when you have money to invest.

Parenthood

You will be sensitive and caring with your children, but may tend to be hypercritical. Help them to develop their imaginations and creative abilities by expressing your own. It should not be hard for you to keep up with your children's ideas and thus avoid the generation gap.

THE MOON IN
LIBRA

PISCES AND LIBRA ARE GENTLE SIGNS. YOU COULD FEIGN A VERY
CALM ATTITUDE WHEN MAKING DECISIONS. TRY TO
MAKE AN EFFORT TO DEVELOP A MORE PRACTICAL APPROACH
TO LIFE, OR YOU MAY NOT FEEL FULFILLED.

The effect of both Pisces and Libra can be to make their subjects charming, friendly, kind, and very sympathetic. You show gentle understanding when challenged or confronted, but may not be eager to make essential snap decisions.

Self-expression

You should consciously try to be more forthright and assertive, and perhaps also more rational and constructively self-critical.

You are diplomatic and always have time for other people, especially if they are upset or in trouble. You have the knack of relaxing them and making them feel much better.

Your Sun and Moon sign combination does not give you a great deal of inner strength, although it is perfectly possible that the influence of other planets within the Solar System have strengthened your psychological muscle.

Romance

You are probably extremely romantic and have a tendency to fall in love with love itself. You may well not feel psychologically whole until you are sharing an emotional relationship.

You are very attractive to the opposite sex, and capable of enjoying a highly rewarding love and sex life.

Your well-being

The lumbar region of the back is ruled by Libra, and you may therefore benefit from an ergonomic chair. The Libran organ is the kidneys, and it is possible that you suffer from an above-average number of headaches. Pressure from other people may provoke these but, if this is not the case, it will be well worth getting a checkup, just in case you have a slight problem with your kidneys.

You probably loathe exercise, but may put on weight if you avoid it completely. Try to be disciplined

The Moon in Libra

about this and about what you eat. Do remember that too much smoking, drinking, or any kind of negative escapism is not good for you. Also note that you can react very badly to many drugs.

Planning ahead

You enjoy your creature comforts, so much of the money that you make probably slips too easily through your fingers. It would be wise for you to follow a savings plan in which a regular payment is deducted from your salary. You are also so generous that some people may seek to take advantage of you. Seek professional advice in all money matters.

Parenthood

You will be a very easygoing parent, and your children will discover that they can manipulate you. They will appreciate your tremendous kindness and sympathy, but remember that children also benefit from a certain amount of discipline. The generation gap should not prove to be a problem.

THE MOON IN
SCORPIO

BOTH PISCES AND SCORPIO ARE SIGNS OF THE WATER ELEMENT,
WHICH WILL HEIGHTEN YOUR ALREADY ABUNDANT PISCEAN
EMOTIONS. LET DETERMINATION OVERCOME INHIBITION AND
ANY LACK OF SELF-CONFIDENCE. SUPPRESS JEALOUSY.

Scorpio is, in many respects, the strongest of the 12 Zodiac signs. Since it is of the water element, its influence blends well with that of your Sun sign.

Self-expression
In addition to your Piscean qualities, you have further inner strength, and considerable resilience and determination when faced with a challenge or a demanding situation. These qualities encourage you to overcome any Piscean reticence, shyness, or lack of self-confidence.

You need to be emotionally involved with your work. While you enjoy making money, it is still more important for you to obtain inner satisfaction from your job.

Romance
You are highly sexed and very passionate. You need an energetic partner who can match your passion,

who will challenge you and keep you stimulated. The worst Scorpio fault is jealousy, and you may sometimes succumb to it. Bear in mind that you could create a somewhat claustrophobic atmosphere within your relationship.

Your well-being
The Scorpio body area covers the genitals. Male Scorpios should therefore regularly examine their testicles for malformations, and women should have cervical smears.

Those with a Scorpio emphasis love good food and wine, and are therefore likely to gain weight. Moderation is the best solution to this problem.

Planning ahead
You will probably cope well with money; much better, in fact, than many Sun sign Pisceans. You may have a certain financial flair, but could tend to put too many eggs in a single

The Moon in Scorpio

basket. If you feel that this tendency
is likely to affect you, you should go
for safe savings plans and, if you are
feeling adventurous, seek professional
financial advice.

Although many Scorpio types
manage to do well in their own
businesses, they sometimes get rather
bored, make an attempt to organize a
change, and finally end up going too
far. In the end they are faced with no
real choice but to start again at the
very bottom.

Parenthood

While Pisces is likely to make you a
kind and easygoing parent, your
Scorpio Moon encourages you to be
much stricter. This is fine, since it
enables you to give your children a
good, secure background. You will,
however, probably have to make a
conscious effort to learn about your
children's concerns and problems if
you are to avoid running into the
many problems associated with the
generation gap.

THE MOON IN
SAGITTARIUS

BEFORE NEPTUNE WAS DISCOVERED, THE PLANET JUPITER RULED
BOTH SAGITTARIUS AND PISCES. THERE IS THEREFORE A
NATURAL SYMPATHY BETWEEN THEM, WHICH IS HEIGHTENED BY
THE FACT THAT THEY ARE DUAL AND MUTABLE SIGNS.

Many Sagittarians respond to challenges in a lively, optimistic, and enthusiastic way. In fact they thrive on them and derive a great deal of excitement from them.

Self-expression

Although you are very good at grasping the overall view of any situation, you could find the details terribly boring. You have a tremendous zest for life and enjoy action more than many Pisceans. Your outlook is philosophical, and you have an admirable mind that should always be engaged in study of some kind, perhaps of a foreign language.

Romance

You have the positive, fiery emotion of Sagittarius, as well as the more sensitive emotion of Pisces. They combine well when it comes to love and sex. You could well have something of a roving eye, and will

certainly get a lot of fun out of this sphere of your life. You tend to fall in and out of love rather often, but will take a broken heart in your stride and readily accept the challenge of finding someone new.

Once you have settled down, other factors come into play, and you will get great satisfaction from a rewarding love and sex life with a partner who is also a good friend.

Your well-being

The Sagittarian body area covers the hips and thighs, and women with this sign emphasized are more than likely to put on weight in those areas. The Sagittarian organ is the liver, and hangovers are often common, so keep a remedy on hand.

A preference for rather heavy dishes and good wine and beer can mean a buildup of weight, so follow your Sagittarian Moon and keep up with sports. Riding is traditionally a

The Moon in Sagittarius

Sagittarian form of exercise. Restlessness is the worst Sagittarian fault. You should try to curb it, or it will lead to stress and tension because of feelings of unfulfillment. Alternating from physical to mental interests and vice versa provides an excellent antidote.

Planning ahead

It is important for you to seek financial advice when you want to start an investment or savings plan. Being a Piscean soft touch is one thing, but having a Sagittarian inclination to take a gamble is quite another. You could fall very easily for get-rich-quick schemes. If you must place a bet, never stake more money than you can easily afford to lose.

Parenthood

You will be an enthusiastic parent and will be extremely eager to encourage your children to stimulate their minds. In addition to this, you will have a great deal of fun with them, and should have almost no difficulty in keeping up with their ideas. The specter of the generation gap should therefore hold no real terrors for you.

THE MOON IN
CAPRICORN

YOU HAVE HIGH ASPIRATIONS, BUT YOUR SENSITIVE PISCEAN SUN
SIGN COULD INHIBIT PROGRESS. BE SELF-CONFIDENT AND
AMBITIOUS, AND FOLLOW YOUR INSTINCTS. THEY MAY WELL BE
MORE PRACTICALLY FOUNDED THAN YOU REALIZE.

The elements of water, for Pisces, and earth, for Capricorn, blend well and give you some very positive common sense.

Self-expression
When challenged, you could be somewhat overcautious. This is fine for a Sun sign Piscean, provided that your natural caution does not sap your self-confidence. To avoid this, set yourself ambitious but attainable objectives, and make sure that you continually aspire to meet every one of them.

There is another side to the Capricornian influence, which could cause you to grumble or to take a negative view of life. Try not to let this tendency get the better of you.

Romance
Your Capricornian Moon prevents you from being gullible in your love life, and you are less likely than many

Pisceans to don rose-colored spectacles when falling in love. Capricorn is not a sign that bestows a high emotional level; Pisces, on the other hand, gives you a capacity to express emotion forcefully towards a partner. You are probably very faithful and eager to see your partner progress in life. Possibly more than most people, you need security within your relationship. You will work really hard for this and do everything in your power to make it work. Do not allow feelings of inferiority to creep into your attitude.

Your well-being
The Capricornian body area covers the knees and shins, as well as the bones, teeth, and skin. It is important for you to get exercise to keep you moving. Jogging, aerobics, or even walking will ensure that you keep rheumatic pains and stiffness of the joints, especially in the knees, at bay.

The Moon in Capricorn

Your skin could be rather sensitive, whatever your race, and it is best to protect it from the sun. You should also have regular dental checkups.

Most people with a Capricornian influence are not heavy eaters. Provided that your Piscean influence does not make you lazy, you should have no problems with your weight.

Planning ahead
You probably cope fairly well with money, although you may have a tendency to think that you are less well-off than you really are. You must get value for your money, so seek financial advice when investing.

Parenthood
You will be a kind, understanding parent and will discipline your children fairly whenever it is necessary. Be careful to avoid undue criticism or put-downs, and allow your tender Sun sign qualities plenty of expression. If you listen to your children, you will leap across the generation gap.

THE MOON IN
AQUARIUS

YOU ARE ALL EMOTION, BUT THE COOL DETACHMENT OF AQUARIUS
WHICH COLORS YOUR REACTIONS MAY MAKE YOU APPEAR A
LITTLE BRITTLE. YOUR SENSITIVE, CHARITABLE PISCEAN WARMTH
USUALLY EMERGES WHEN PEOPLE GET TO KNOW YOU.

The tender warmth of Pisces is contrasted in a very vivid and exciting way against the cool glamour and originality of Aquarius. When challenged, you find it easy to distance yourself from a problem and to respond logically.

Self-expression
You may sometimes give the impression of being cool and distant. However, once people get to know you, they discover a very different person. Aquarius is known for general friendliness and kind, humanitarian qualities, and Pisces for charity. You will therefore give a great deal of yourself to people in need.

Romance
You are a very caring, loving, and tender partner with a high emotional level. While you are extremely attractive to the opposite sex, you may distance yourself when you feel that a prospective lover is pressing you too fast. You have a very independent streak that may well influence your whole lifestyle. Perhaps you have built a life that is in some way unique. If this is the case, do not allow yourself to be pressured into changing it. Aim to achieve a rewarding love and sex life with partners who recognize your strong need for independence.

Your well-being
The Aquarian body area covers the ankles. Because Pisces rules the feet, and since your ankles are vulnerable due to your Moon sign's influence, you need to make sure that you always buy comfortable footwear.

The circulation is also ruled by Aquarius but, while you may feel the cold fairly easily, you also enjoy cold, clear winter weather. Make sure that you keep warm by wearing several layers of light clothing.

The Moon in Aquarius

It is advisable for you to try to get aesthetic satisfaction from exercise, so that your mind, body, and spirit will be at one. You also need to keep moving because of possible circulation problems. You could well be a natural iceskater, skier, or synchronized swimmer.

Planning ahead
Coping with money may not be very easy for you – unless other planets within the Solar System contribute a positive influence to this sphere. You may spend heavily on glamorous items. Always seek professional advice before investing.

Parenthood
Your attitude toward your children may be unconventional. You have plenty of ideas about bringing them up; make sure they always know where they stand. You look to the future, so the generation gap should not trouble you.

THE MOON IN
PISCES

BECAUSE THE SUN AND THE MOON WERE BOTH IN PISCES AT THE
MOMENT OF YOUR BIRTH, YOU WERE BORN UNDER A FULL
MOON. SINCE PISCES IS A WATER SIGN, THIS ELEMENT POWERFULLY
INFLUENCES YOUR PERSONALITY AND REACTIONS.

When you read a list of the characteristics of your sensitive and emotional Sun sign, you will probably recognize that many of them apply to you. On average, out of a list of perhaps 20 personality traits attached to a Sun sign, most people identify with 11 or 12. For you the average increases greatly, since the Sun and the Moon were both in Pisces when you were born.

Self-expression

Your Sun sign makes you highly imaginative and gives you some very powerful emotions; because the Moon was also in Pisces when you were born, you will sometimes react very emotionally to situations.

Far more than most Sun sign Pisceans, you will be inclined to decide on one line of action, and then do the opposite. As a result of this, you may cause yourself a considerable amount of worry and confusion.

Romance

You will give a great deal of yourself to your lovers and readily make sacrifices for them. Think about this, and make sure that you do not compromise too often.

You want a good, stable relationship and a partner who will encourage and support you, spurring you on to express your potential. You are a very sensual lover, and will enjoy a rich and rewarding sex life with your partner. It is possible that you fall in love too easily, and you could well deceive yourself about your lovers' qualities, ignoring their faults and foibles. Be cautious in this sphere.

Your well-being

The comments made on pages 22 to 23 about Piscean health and well-being really do apply to you. You can hardly escape having problem feet and must recognize their great vulnerability. Only go barefoot in the

The Moon in Pisces

house; otherwise you will pick up foot infections very easily. Also watch your eating habits. Many Pisceans are prone to weight gain, and this tendency will probably affect you more than most. Although you may not be enthusiastic about the idea, you should discipline yourself in the way that you eat, and make sure that you take regular exercise.

Planning ahead
In regard to money, the less you have to do with balancing your books the better. This may be something that a partner should take care of. If you

have money to invest, then get professional advice. If you have a regular income, embark on a savings plan in which contributions can be deducted at the source.

Parenthood
You may find disciplining your children rather difficult, and you could spoil them. For their sakes, and your own peace of mind, work on disciplining them when they start to grow up. Because you have an instinctive understanding of human nature, you should have no problems with the generation gap.

MOON CHARTS

REFER TO THE FOLLOWING TABLES TO DISCOVER YOUR MOON SIGN.
THE PRECEDING PAGES WILL TELL YOU ABOUT ITS QUALITIES.

By referring to the charts on pages 57, 58 and 59 locate the Zodiacal glyph for the month of the year in which you were born. Using the Moon table on this page, find the number opposite the day you were born that month. Then, starting from the glyph you found first, count off that number using the list of Zodiacal glyphs (below, right). You may have to count to Pisces and continue with Aries. For example, if you were born on May 21, 1991, first you need to find the Moon sign on the chart on page 59. Look down the chart to May; the glyph is

Sagittarius (♐). Then consult the Moon table for the 21st. It tells you to add nine glyphs. Starting from Sagittarius, count down nine, and you find your Moon sign is Virgo (♍).

Note that because the Moon moves so quickly, it is beyond the scope of this little book to provide a detailed chart of its positions. For more detailed horoscopes, you will need to consult an astrologer, but if you feel that this chart gives a result that does not seem to apply to you, read the pages for the signs either before or after the one indicated; one of the three will apply.

MOON TABLE

DAYS OF THE MONTH AND NUMBER OF SIGNS THAT SHOULD BE ADDED

DAY	ADD	DAY	ADD	DAY	ADD	DAY	ADD
1	0	9	4	17	7	25	11
2	1	10	4	18	8	26	11
3	1	11	5	19	8	27	12
4	1	12	5	20	9	28	12
5	2	13	5	21	9	29	1
6	2	14	6	22	10	30	1
7	3	15	6	23	10	31	2
8	3	16	7	24	10		

ZODIACAL GLYPHS

♈	Aries
♉	Taurus
♊	Gemini
♋	Cancer
♌	Leo
♍	Virgo
♎	Libra
♏	Scorpio
♐	Sagittarius
♑	Capricorn
♒	Aquarius
♓	Pisces

	1923	1924	1925	1926	1927	1928	1929	1930	1931	1932	1933	1934	1935
JAN	♊	♏	♈	♌	♐	♈	♍	♑	♉	♎	♓	♋	♏
FEB	♌	♐	♉	♍	♑	♊	♏	♓	♋	♐	♈	♌	♑
MAR	♌	♑	♉	♍	♒	♋	♏	♓	♋	♐	♉	♍	♑
APR	♎	♓	♋	♏	♈	♍	♑	♉	♍	♒	♊	♎	♓
MAY	♏	♈	♌	♐	♉	♎	♒	♊	♎	♓	♋	♐	♈
JUN	♑	♉	♍	♒	♋	♏	♓	♌	♐	♉	♍	♑	♊
JUL	♒	♋	♏	♓	♌	♐	♈	♍	♑	♊	♎	♓	♋
AUG	♈	♌	♐	♉	♍	♒	♊	♏	♓	♋	♐	♈	♌
SEP	♉	♎	♒	♋	♏	♓	♌	♐	♈	♍	♑	♊	♎
OCT	♊	♏	♓	♌	♐	♉	♍	♑	♉	♎	♓	♋	♏
NOV	♌	♑	♉	♍	♑	♊	♏	♓	♋	♐	♈	♌	♑
DEC	♍	♒	♊	♎	♓	♌	♐	♈	♌	♑	♉	♍	♒

	1936	1937	1938	1939	1940	1941	1942	1943	1944	1945	1946	1947	1948
JAN	♈	♌	♑	♉	♍	♒	♊	♎	♓	♌	♐	♈	♍
FEB	♉	♎	♒	♊	♏	♈	♌	♐	♉	♍	♑	♊	♎
MAR	♊	♎	♒	♋	♐	♈	♌	♐	♉	♎	♒	♉	♏
APR	♌	♐	♈	♌	♑	♉	♎	♒	♋	♏	♓	♌	♑
MAY	♍	♑	♉	♎	♒	♊	♏	♓	♌	♐	♉	♍	♒
JUN	♎	♒	♋	♏	♈	♌	♑	♉	♎	♒	♊	♏	♓
JUL	♏	♈	♌	♑	♉	♍	♒	♊	♏	♓	♌	♐	♈
AUG	♑	♉	♎	♒	♋	♏	♈	♌	♐	♉	♍	♑	♊
SEP	♓	♋	♏	♈	♌	♑	♉	♍	♒	♋	♏	♓	♌
OCT	♈	♌	♑	♉	♎	♒	♊	♎	♓	♌	♐	♈	♍
NOV	♊	♎	♒	♊	♏	♈	♌	♐	♉	♍	♑	♊	♏
DEC	♋	♏	♓	♌	♑	♉	♍	♑	♊	♎	♒	♋	♐

	1949	1950	1951	1952	1953	1954	1955	1956	1957	1958	1959	1960	1961
JAN	♑	♊	♎	♓	♋	♏	♈	♌	♑	♉	♍	♒	♋
FEB	♓	♋	♐	♈	♍	♑	♉	♎	♒	♊	♏	♈	♌
MAR	♓	♋	♐	♉	♍	♑	♊	♏	♓	♋	♍	♈	♌
APR	♉	♍	♒	♊	♎	♓	♋	♐	♈	♌	♑	♊	♎
MAY	♊	♎	♓	♋	♐	♈	♍	♑	♉	♎	♒	♋	♏
JUN	♌	♐	♈	♍	♑	♊	♎	♓	♋	♐	♈	♌	♑
JUL	♍	♑	♊	♎	♓	♋	♏	♈	♌	♑	♉	♍	♒
AUG	♏	♓	♋	♐	♈	♍	♑	♉	♎	♒	♊	♏	♈
SEP	♐	♈	♍	♑	♊	♎	♒	♋	♐	♈	♌	♑	♊
OCT	♑	♊	♎	♓	♋	♏	♓	♌	♑	♉	♍	♒	♋
NOV	♓	♋	♏	♈	♍	♑	♉	♎	♒	♊	♏	♈	♌
DEC	♈	♌	♑	♊	♎	♒	♊	♏	♓	♌	♐	♉	♍

	1962	1963	1964	1965	1966	1967	1968	1969	1970	1971	1972	1973	1974
JAN	♏	♓	♌	♐	♈	♍	♑	♊	♎	♒	♋	♐	♈
FEB	♐	♉	♍	♒	♊	♏	♓	♋	♏	♈	♍	♑	♉
MAR	♐	♉	♎	♒	♊	♏	♈	♌	♐	♉	♍	♑	♊
APR	♒	♋	♏	♈	♐	♑	♉	♍	♒	♊	♏	♓	♋
MAY	♓	♌	♐	♉	♍	♒	♊	♎	♓	♋	♐	♈	♍
JUN	♉	♎	♒	♊	♏	♓	♌	♐	♉	♍	♑	♊	♎
JUL	♊	♏	♓	♌	♐	♈	♍	♑	♊	♎	♓	♋	♐
AUG	♌	♐	♉	♎	♒	♊	♏	♓	♋	♏	♈	♍	♑
SEP	♍	♒	♋	♏	♓	♋	♐	♉	♍	♑	♊	♎	♓
OCT	♏	♓	♌	♐	♈	♍	♒	♊	♎	♒	♋	♐	♈
NOV	♐	♉	♎	♒	♊	♎	♓	♋	♐	♈	♍	♑	♉
DEC	♑	♊	♏	♓	♋	♐	♈	♌	♑	♉	♎	♒	♊

	1975	1976	1977	1978	1979	1980	1981	1982	1983	1984	1985	1986	1987
JAN	♌	♑	♉	♍	♒	♊	♏	♓	♌	♐	♉	♍	♑
FEB	♎	♒	♋	♏	♈	♌	♐	♉	♍	♒	♊	♎	♓
MAR	♎	♓	♋	♏	♈	♍	♑	♉	♎	♒	♊	♏	♓
APR	♐	♈	♍	♑	♊	♎	♒	♋	♏	♈	♌	♑	♉
MAY	♑	♉	♎	♒	♋	♏	♓	♌	♐	♉	♍	♒	♊
JUN	♓	♋	♐	♈	♌	♑	♉	♎	♒	♊	♏	♓	♌
JUL	♈	♌	♑	♉	♍	♒	♋	♏	♓	♌	♐	♉	♍
AUG	♉	♎	♓	♋	♏	♈	♌	♐	♈	♎	♒	♊	♎
SEP	♋	♐	♈	♌	♐	♊	♎	♒	♊	♏	♓	♌	♐
OCT	♌	♑	♉	♍	♒	♋	♏	♓	♋	♐	♉	♍	♑
NOV	♎	♓	♋	♏	♓	♌	♐	♉	♍	♒	♊	♎	♓
DEC	♏	♈	♌	♐	♉	♍	♑	♊	♎	♓	♋	♐	♈

	1988	1989	1990	1991	1992	1993	1994	1995	1996	1997	1998	1999	2000
JAN	♊	♎	♒	♋	♏	♈	♌	♑	♉	♎	♒	♊	♏
FEB	♋	♐	♈	♍	♑	♉	♎	♒	♋	♏	♈	♌	♐
MAR	♌	♐	♉	♍	♒	♊	♎	♓	♋	♏	♈	♌	♑
APR	♍	♒	♊	♏	♓	♋	♐	♈	♍	♑	♊	♎	♓
MAY	♏	♓	♌	♐	♈	♍	♑	♉	♎	♒	♋	♏	♈
JUN	♐	♉	♍	♑	♊	♎	♓	♋	♐	♈	♌	♑	♉
JUL	♑	♊	♎	♒	♋	♐	♈	♌	♑	♉	♎	♒	♋
AUG	♓	♌	♐	♈	♍	♑	♉	♎	♓	♋	♏	♓	♌
SEP	♉	♍	♑	♊	♏	♓	♋	♏	♈	♌	♑	♉	♎
OCT	♊	♎	♒	♋	♐	♈	♌	♑	♉	♎	♒	♊	♏
NOV	♌	♐	♈	♍	♑	♉	♎	♒	♋	♏	♈	♌	♑
DEC	♍	♑	♉	♎	♒	♋	♏	♈	♌	♐	♉	♍	♒

THE
SOLAR SYSTEM

THE STARS, OTHER THAN THE SUN, PLAY NO PART IN THE SCIENCE OF ASTROLOGY. ASTROLOGERS USE ONLY THE BODIES IN THE SOLAR SYSTEM, EXCLUDING THE EARTH, TO CALCULATE HOW OUR LIVES AND PERSONALITIES CHANGE.

Pluto
Pluto takes 246 years to travel around the Sun. It affects our unconscious instincts and urges, gives us strength in difficulty, and perhaps emphasizes any inherent cruel streak.

Neptune
Neptune stays in each sign for 14 years. At best it makes us sensitive and imaginative; at worst it encourages deceit and carelessness, making us worry.

Uranus
The influence of Uranus can make us friendly, kind, eccentric, inventive, and unpredictable.

Saturn
In ancient times, Saturn was the most distant known planet. Its influence can limit our ambition and make us either overly cautious (but practical), or reliable and self-disciplined.

PLUTO

NEPTUNE

URANUS

SATURN

Jupiter

Jupiter encourages expansion, optimism, generosity, and breadth of vision. It can, however, also make us wasteful, extravagant, and conceited.

Mars

Much associated with energy, anger, violence, selfishness, and a strong sex drive, Mars also encourages decisiveness and leadership.

JUPITER

The Moon

Although it is a satellite of the Earth, the Moon is known in astrology as a planet. It lies about 240,000 miles from the Earth and, astrologically, is second in importance to the Sun.

MERCURY

THE MOON

VENUS

MARS EARTH

The Sun

The Sun, the only star used by astrologers, influences the way we present ourselves to the world – our image or personality; the face we show to other people.

Venus

The planet of love and partnership, Venus can emphasize all our best personal qualities. It may also encourage us to be lazy, impractical, and too dependent on other people.

Earth

Every planet contributes to the environment of the Solar System, and a person born on Venus would no doubt be influenced by our own planet in some way.

Mercury

The planet closest to the Sun affects our intellect. It can make us inquisitive, versatile, argumentative, perceptive, and clever, but maybe also inconsistent, cynical, and sarcastic.